Precious Memories

14 Daily Devotions

James Wertz

IHP Practica
West Frankfort, Illinois

IHP Practica
An Imprint of Illative House Press, LLC
500 E. Elm St.
West Frankfort, IL 62896
IllativeHousePress.com

Paperback ISBN: 979-8-9873886-6-2

Cover Design: Illative House Press
Cover Image: Original painting by Dmarie Holder; used by permission.

Unless otherwise noted, Scripture quotations are from the New King James Version.

Contents

Publisher's Preface

Part of the vision of Illative House Press, and an important part, is creating opportunities for writers from across the Christian community. We firmly believe that when God calls and gifts someone to write, that calling and those gifts demand and deserve an opportunity. James Wertz is one whom God called and gifted to write, and I'm delighted to see how his calling and gifts continue to develop. For this reason, I was eager to see James' third book, *Precious Memories*, come to fruition and become the first publication of our IHP Practica imprint. The mission of IHP Practica is to promote works dedicated to practical Christian living, and practical Christian living is what motivates James.

In working with authors in the IHP family, it is vital that our editorial process enhances and never hinders their unique voice and style. Our hope is that James' voice and style come through clearly in the pages that follow. He writes as he talks, and he talks in a direct and plain-spoken manner. His life experience comes through in his writing, and his insights are many and varied. I trust that you will find yourself drawn closer to God as you read and reflect on James' devotional offerings and that you encounter on a deeper level the one James is fond of describing as, "My Jesus."

T. J. Gentry
President and Founder
Illative House Press

Foreword

I wish I could say that every day of my Christian life has been spent in close fellowship with our Savior. But the truth is, there have been moments when God felt incredibly close, and moments when He felt far away. The moments God felt farthest away were dark ones. It felt like the events of my life--my struggles, my losses, my pain—didn't matter to God, or at least, didn't matter very much. As I worked through those feelings of separation, I found that two things were always true. First, God wasn't the one who had moved away—I was. It turns out that God can't pull away, ever. His very nature is to be next to me, with me, part of me. Part of you too. Second, the road back to God always begins with my first step toward Him. Why did I wait so long?

How do we become distant from God? More importantly, how do we ensure that we never do? The Bible is helpful as always—particularly the writings of the Apostle Paul. Paul highlights three things that assure our constant closeness to God: Daily prayer (1 Thessalonians 5:17), daily study in Scripture (2 Timothy 2:15), and regular fellowship with other Christians (Hebrews 10: 24-25). These three seem simple enough but how do we maintain them when our job keeps us constantly traveling and away from our Christian friends and support network?

That's where *Precious Memories* comes in. In fact, that's where the ministry of James Wertz comes in. In this book, and others, James provides Scripturally based devotionals that you can perform anywhere. Each devotional includes biblical references and a set of questions for you to reflect on and work through. This one little book provides a focused way to study

Scripture, pray, and interact with James through his questions. This one little book helps you to never become distant from God.

Finally, note that the devotionals are on different topics—each relevant to everyday living. Also note that the devotionals are linked to a theme found in Isaiah 64:8: *"But now O LORD, You are our Father; we are the clay, and You our potter; and all we are the work of Your hand."* God is our Father and potter, and we are the clay. If we stay close to Him, He will shape each of us into a masterpiece. Please enjoy these devotionals.

Walter McFarland
Founder, The National Unity Project

1. A Pile of Lumber, a Pile of Clay

Over the years, I've noticed that the pulpit, any pulpit's workmanship, is of the highest quality, with no visible flaws or defects. Pulpits are beautiful, and at the·same time, there seems to be a mystery about them. They have a solid stand-alone look as well as an inviting look and a look of demanding respect. But at the same time a very humbling look. I've always wondered about the carpenter who took the time and skills to build something so beautiful and strong looking out of nothing more than a pile of lumber. I wonder when he started, if he had any idea what it would look like when finished. Or did he use plans from someone else, or did he just build it? Now think about the man, any man, who every Sunday morning stands behind the pulpit and brings a message that God has laid upon his heart. Just as the pulpit started as a pile of lumber this man standing behind the pulpit started as a pile of clay. But God took this pile of clay and molded it into someone, a teacher/preacher to bring His message to feed His sheep and to lead them.

Isaiah 64:8

But now O LORD, You are our Father; we are the clay, and You our potter; and all we are the work of Your hand.

Think about it this way. We all started out as a pile of clay. But God took that pile of clay and shaped each one of us differently…agreed? While we are all not called to be teachers/preachers and to lead a church, we are all in our own ways, called to feed His people just the same. The one standing behind the pulpit is tasked with teaching us how to go about feeding God's people. And our task is to take what we've heard and learned and go about the task given to us. Whatever

God has molded you into we must give it our best and nothing less…agreed? Maybe some of us wish we had been called as a teacher/preacher but remember this: this calling comes with greater responsibility and harsher judgment. Are those shoes you want to try and fill, no matter who you are? As God molds us into the person He wants us to be, we could find ourselves instead of sitting in the back of the room and being comfortable, standing right beside the preacher, at the front of the room. And just as easily, could end up with a ministry just as strong as the preacher's even though we're not a preacher. With God being the potter and molding the clay (that's us) we just don't know what'll happen. But if we are willing and allow God to lead us, who knows what can happen?

James 3:1

My brethren, let not many of you become teachers, knowing that we shall receive a stricter judgment.

I've talked about how God molds us out of clay into what we are today. Do you feel like God is finished with molding you or is He still at work with you? I believe it is an ongoing task and that God is never finished molding us. Or never finished with what or which task He is going to have us fulfill. Agree or disagree? For myself, I've always felt like a "poster child" for the saying, "God calls the unqualified and makes them qualified." The passage in 1 Corinthians 1:25-31 comes to mind when I'm thinking about people whom God has placed in the position of teaching/preaching and leaders in a church. I'm going to highlight a couple of verses, not all of them.

1 Corinthians 1:25-27

Because the foolishness of God is wiser than men, and the weakness of God is stronger than men. For you see your calling, brethren, that not many wise according to the flesh, not many mighty, not many noble, are called. But God has chosen the foolish things of the world to put to shame the wise, and God has chosen the weak things of the world to put to shame the things which are mighty.

One of the reasons I like this passage is because it tells us that no matter how smart we think we are, it's nothing compared to what God has in store for each and every one of us and the wisdom He has. So just as the carpenter takes a pile of lumber and builds a beautiful pulpit, we need to allow God to take the pile of clay that we are and mold us into the vision He has for us.

Questions for Further Reflection

As God molds us, is there anything we need to be doing as this work in being done to us?

Do you agree or disagree that God will mold some into being nothing more than a leader in the church, such as an Elder or Deacon?

Who should teach the younger men and women how to become leaders in the church? What are some of the ways we can do this?

2. Whose Child Is This?

I'm going to share with you about two women I know, both of whom have a strong walk in Christ. The first overcame a tough childhood. Growing up, she heard very few words of encouragement, if any, just the opposite. She has told me that she heard nothing but nasty comments and how she'll never amount to anything; these are words that hurt and are hard to overcome. But she managed to overcome her rough childhood, but it wasn't easy. As she grew, she did her best to surround herself with people who could help her achieve her desired life. By doing so, she also became very successful in her career field. She never went to college, but she finished high school. She's a hard worker and doesn't know the word "quit." She instilled these qualities in her children as well. Having raised her children, she has now taken in a child who was going to end up having a rough childhood just like she had. Knowing what lay ahead for this child, she didn't want the child to experience that life. So, she and her husband opened their home to take this child in and raise it so the child could have a fighting chance.

Now, the second lady I know grew up in a Christian home filled with love and every opportunity one could think of. Her parents have a strong walk in Christ that they passed on to their children. But when this young lady married and tried to start a family, she discovered she could not have children. Most women don't want to hear this. So, she and her husband decided to become foster parents and they have had a number of kids pass through their home. This couple has been able to adopt a couple of the kids, so they have a family. But she didn't stop there, they still open their home to kids who need a home for any amount of time. And she encourages people to become foster parents. While these kids are staying at her home, she and her husband take them to church and teach them about the love of Christ. And her parents are just as involved with helping raise these kids as much as possible. Showing them the love that grandparents have and can give to children who are not their own.

Two different women raised totally different but willing to take in children who need a home and love. When I hear of people like these two women it gives me encouragement to do better as a Christian. But it also raises some questions, like? What or who made such an impression on them that they would undertake a task as big as what they're doing? I know both ladies and for one thing they are doing this out of love for the children and also for the love they have for God and not for praise and glory. Because they know their reward is yet to come. But I also believe they're not really worried about any rewards just serving their Savior. And being able to raise children who will love the Lord as they do. These two ladies remind me of a verse in...

Isaiah 64:8

But now O LORD, You are our Father; we are the clay, and You our potter; and all we are the work of Your hand.

I can remember as a teenage my grandmother who was a Godly woman, sitting in her rocking chair slowing rocking back and forth singing "Rock of Ages." Wall looking out the window seemingly lost in her own little world. I never really understood at the time why. But as I get older, I understand why. Have you ever thought about the people in our lives and the impact they have? Big or small it doesn't matter. It doesn't matter if it's someone we've known a lifetime or just a short time. God passes people through our lives for many reasons.

Sometimes it's to help the one passing through. And other times the one passing through helps us in any number of ways.

But I'm also learning from these two ladies' examples in how they are molding these children, we should be doing the same if given a chance. I'm sure it's very scary and at times overwhelming when mentoring a child who is not yours. But if God has placed that child in your care, He's not expecting anything less, right? And by the same means if someone comes to us asking us to help them grow in their walk in Christ. We should, right?

Questions for Further Reflection

What are some of the ways we as adults can mentor children?

Are children able to mentor other children? If so, how? And do you think a child can mentor or teach an adult? If so, how? If not, how come?

Would you be willing to take a child into your home, as these two ladies are doing? I understand not everyone can do this. But if you could, would you?

3. Making of Church Leaders

Some men are born to become leaders. Some will lead the church, and others choose to manage a company instead. How does one decide which they'd like to lead? Has anyone ever thought about the difference, or is there any difference? If you're the CEO of a business, you only have to answer to a Broad of Directors or the stockholders. And if you mess up, you get fired and move on to another company to run. Possibly get a nice pay package when your services are no longer needed.

I was thinking about this the other day because it was in the church bulletin about how it's time to nominate men for Deacon and Elders. These are positions of leadership in the church that cannot and should not be taken lightly. Being a Deacon is where you start learning about leadership in the church. The Deacons, Elders, and Ministers start molding you to help you grow if you want to become a leader in the church. You work more closely with the Elders and slowly learn about church leadership. And you start to understand the meaning of…

James 3:1

My brethren, let not many of you become teachers, knowing that we shall receive a stricter judgment.

So, being a leader in the church, I believe, holds a greater responsibility than being a CEO of a business. If you get fired from a business, it's no big deal. But lead the church and its people who are God's children astray now that's a big deal, and Scripture tells us as much. It's so important that the Elders and the Minister of the church teach and mold the young men into becoming strong leaders of the church for the future. I don't mean strong like being a dictator towards the Congregation, but strong in the knowledge of Scripture and leading with a firm but gentle touch. If the older men don't mold and teach the younger men how to become leaders in the church, they will have let them down. They've also let themselves and the church down.

If you wish to be a CEO at a business, you work your way up from the bottom. Or go to college and earn a degree. Or your parents own the company, and you wait until it's your turn — nothing like that in filling leadership roles in the church. Scripture tells us the qualifications and how Elders are to lead the congregation. The book of Titus 1:5-16 outlines what qualities a man should have to accept this role of Elder. As an individual, when reading the qualifications outlined, you began to see the seriousness of the role of the Elder in the church. And when you think about what James 3:1 says, many men choose not to serve in this role of church leader. And there is nothing wrong with that; not every man is meant to be a Deacon or Elder in the church. But they can still lead and mold people in other ways and be just as effective. Because this is a decision most men struggle with. When making this decision, one begins to see the seriousness of church leadership and the responsibility involved.

As you pray about a decision like this, more than likely, you are seeking guidance from the Minister and the Elders in making this decision. You will have learned this from leadership spending time molding you and helping you to understand how church leadership works. Church leadership is not about power over the congregation, but it's about leading by example. And 1 Peter 5:1-3 tells how the Elders are to lead the congregation. Wall, this passage tells men how to guide. I believe Luke 15:4-7 is equally essential to what we're talking about. Let's look at verse four:

What man of you, having a hundred sheep, if he loses one of them, does not leave the ninety-nine in the wilderness, and go after the one which is lost until he finds it?

Church leadership is equally responsible for the one who strays away as they are for the congregation. When church leadership goes after the one who's lost their way, it shows the congregation that leadership is more worried about feeding the congregation and caring for their needs than anything else. But this type of leadership only comes about because older men in the congregation are willing to mold and teach the younger men how to lead.

Questions for Further Reflection

Do you think it makes a difference in church attendance based on the leadership in the church? If so, in what ways?

What are some of the ways leadership has molded men in the church to help them grow so that they can become leaders in the church?

What role, if any, do women play in leadership in the church with the younger women?

4. Why? How Could You Do This?

I stood at the back of the funeral home, getting ready to leave. I see the young mother walking up to the casket for a few private moments, knowing that these would be her last minutes with her fiancé. One could only imagine the hurt, pain, and betrayal she was feeling and experiencing. Left with so many unanswered questions, will she ever find the answer? Promises that he made but now can never be kept. The dreams that we talked about are fading away with each passing day. Had you been taken in a car wreck, today would have been easier to understand and deal with. If there had been an accident at work, today would have been easier. But instead, you took your own life, and that's just so hard to deal with and accept and, most of all, understand. And it leaves so many with an empty feeling that, for some, will never be overcome. Why? How could you do this?

1 Corinthians 10:13

No temptation has overtaken you except such as is common to man; but God is faithful, who will not allow you to be tempted beyond what you are able, but with the temptation will also make the way of escape, that you may be able to bear it.

Earlier, I sat and waited for the service to start. I could hear family and friends talking to each other, trying to understand how your life had gotten to this point. Hearing them say…if he'd had only called, we could have talked it out. But not this. Why? Someone else said they were very mad and angry and were having a hard time dealing with today. And it would be a long time before they could understand why. Pain and sorrow for those who loved you as they try and figure this out. Those who had helped you grow from a small child to an adult were proud of who you had become and were looking forward to seeing the life that you were living. Now they too are struggling with today. But I've heard that when someone decides to do something like this to themselves. They have already passed up every chance offered to them to stop something like this from happening. I've never understood how someone could do something like this to themselves and I guess I never will, we never will. Life goes on for those who are left behind with unanswered questions and trying to figure out why; how you could do this?

As a Christian we know that we can come to the Lord with whatever is bringing us down and find comfort in His word or just get on our knees and pray. Or call another believer for someone to talk to that can help us in our time of need. We are never alone and it's never too late, even if you're not a child of God I believe that if you cry out to God, He will hear you and step in to help you. Because John 3:17 basically tells us that Jesus came to save the world and not to judge the world. This is why I believe if you cry out in your time of need, He will answer you. Because basically you've reached bottom. And there is nowhere else to go. but up. The older I get the more I'm understanding this passage in Matthew 11:28-30 and yet at times, like today, it seems as if I can't understand this passage at all.

As I sat and listened to the preacher's message, I wondered how do non-believes deal with life's difficulties, like today. Where do they turn for comfort and strength to get through something like this, the taking of one's own life? We know words offered have little comfort, if any. And a firm handshake or tight hug once released…in a few minutes is gone as well. How will this young mother keep going because the questions are never going away, not even with time. In fact, with time, they could get more difficult to understand and even harder to answers. The broken promises. The dreams that were once talked about have all but vanished. Why? How could you do this?

Matthew 11:28-30

Come to Me, all you who labor and are heavy laden, and I will give you rest. Take My yoke upon you and learn from Me, for I am gentle and lowly in heart, and you will find rest for your souls. For My yoke is easy and My burden is light.

Questions for Further Reflection

How, or maybe, what, can we do to deal with death? Is there a difference in how we would deal with someone who takes their own life as compared to someone who dies from natural causes?

As a Christian if you were to take your own life would that be a sin? Do you feel or believe God would forgive you if you were to do something like this?

What if you were terminally ill with no cure and pain beyond anything you've ever experienced before and nothing to ease the pain? How about then? What about soldiers on a battlefield?

Further Reflection: How I've Grown Over the Years

I was boarding the bus that would take me to St. Louis. And then, later that night, catch the plane that would take me to San Antonio, Texas, for basic training. I remember those days as a young adult ready to take on the world. In my suitcase, besides a change of clothes, I had all the wisdom and teachings my parents had given me to prepare me for this moment in life. We'll, I thought I was prepared as I look back now some forty years later. All I was really doing was entering into the first day of "the school of hard knocks." Because no matter how much my parents prepared me, I had a lot to learn, and life was beginning.

Since writing the above devotion, I've learned a lot and I'm still learning. I'm told this is how we grow, and it could be. But it could also be that what I was taught as a child was wrong. Not that I was taught wrong, but the information taught was wrong. Because science and knowledge changes daily and at times, we can't keep up. There were a couple of people who with their input I was able to write that devotion. And at the same time caused me to think about as I was growing up how mental problems were not understood then, as they are today and were still learning. But at the same time the Mental Health Community still has more to learn and is still learning. Growing up, if someone had mental problems people just said, they're not trying hard enough. Or maybe even, "They're just lazy." And other comments like that. But if you said you were a Christian and had mental problems, it was said. "They lack faith; that's all that's wrong with them." So, we can say that many things caused this narrow thinking. The unknown is what gets each of us every time, the unknown.

One of the individuals whose input helped me also challenged me and I'm going to share some of what they said. Because I believe it's important to show that we're never too old to change how we think about something. Even mental illness as misunderstood as it is and difficult to understand. They said if I reread that devotion that I would see where God would reveal more to me. Truth be told as soon as I finished writing that devotion God was opening my eyes and I've had more question now, then before I wrote it. Will I ever get answers to those questions that I have? I doubt it. But I've learned to be more open minded about things I don't know or understand. One of the things I'm finding out about these devotions that I write, and share. Is the different ways and different effects they have on the person reading them. I'll always seek out others opinion on different topics I write about because I believe that's how we learn, at least for me. Is to seek out people who know and are willing to teach if you're willing to learn. But that's the key...we must be willing to learn.

I normally don't go back and read a devotion I've written because then I'll see I could have written it differently, but not this one. This one I have reread several times, and it always leaves me sad. I believe because I see a life taken too early and lives left in ruins from their action. The lives left behind are now left with the task of trying to put their lives back together and explain something they themselves don't understand and try and move on. But mostly trying to be positive again when it would be so easy to give up and place blame on what has happened to them. I've never experienced something like this in my life and never want to. But at the same time, I'm trying as best I can to understand this...but it's difficult. I felt led to write this devotion and I did as best I could. My prayer is that whoever reads this devotion it'll help them in some small way. One more challenge this person gave me was this: In what way(s) will this be helpful to the reader? More questions to find answers to.

5. Promises Made, Promises Kept

On their special day, the bride and groom are nothing but a bundle of nervous. They have been waiting for this day, to start their new life together. And to share this special moment with family and friends. Everything is in place from the decoration to the food to the music that's going to be played. Special family members are giving the choice seats, so they won't miss anything. If the couple have written their own vows, they've asked the preacher a hundred times if he has them. The bride is double checking everything again and again worried that something will go wrong on this, their special day. The time comes and the young couple is standing before the preacher, friends, family, and God. Words are spoken and promises are made to each other. But with everything going on the couple isn't really listening to the words spoken because their minds are elsewhere at this moment.

Matthew 19:4-6

Have you not read that He who made them at the beginning 'made them male and female,' and said, 'For this reason a man shall leave his father and mother and be joined to his wife, and the two shall become one flesh'? So then, they are no longer two but one flesh. Therefore what God has joined together, let not man separate.

The young couple starts off on life's journey ready to tackle whatever life throws at them. They start a family and do the best they can to raise their children in a Christian home. Life is good. They plan for the future and look forward to the day when they can retire. To enjoy time with grandkids and travel and enjoy life. Enjoy the things they couldn't do when they were younger because of work and raising a family. And then life throws something at this couple they least expected the wife gets sick. All those plans that were made to travel and enjoy retirement are changed their gone. This couple enjoyed playing golf and had plans to play a round of golf at each of their favorite courses. But instead, they now make plans to visit doctor's appointments instead of golf courses. But what's so special about this love story is that the husband took his bride home. A home they had made together. I'm sure it was a home that was full of love and laughter and lots of memories. If he had put her in a nursing home no one would have said anything. In fact, I'm sure people wouldn't have thought less of him. Because after all men are not care givers by nature, men are by God's design are providers. I watched this couple struggle with what life had dealt them and I see how they overcame it as well. I'm sure this man didn't know the impact he was having on those around him. For me he brought to life the verse in Isaiah 64:8:

But now O LORD, You are our Father; we are the clay, and You our potter; and all we are the work of Your hand.

Because watching him in a small but powerful way helped to make me just a little stronger as a husband and father. And it also showed me that men can do things that are not normal for us to do. If you're a newly married man or someone who's been married for several years, there's a lesson to be learned here. We can see firsthand about promises that were made and how they are to be kept. Because after all someone is depending on you. Not just for material things but to know at their lowest most needing time in life, you are there for them. We can be counted on without question. But the one question that we as men are unable to answer at this moment is…can I do this. Take care of my wife if she needs round the clock care. We need to learn to place our trust in our Savior just as this couple had placed their love to each other.

Psalm 56:3-4

Whenever I am afraid, I will trust in You. In God (I will praise His word), in God I have put my trust; I will not fear. What can flesh do to me?

This couple whom I watched and visited with whenever I could I learned so much from. And I'm just guessing but I'm sure others learned as well. You could see in his face and how he moved that taking care of his wife played a heavy toll on his health. So, I can't help but think this verse gave him the strength to continue. Because without words spoken looking back, I see this passage living out in his life.

Questions for Further Reflection

What value have you placed on your wedding vows?

If you were to break a promise that you made to your spouse, would it be the same as breaking a promise made to any other person?

By watching other people, be they married couples or single people, what effect have they had on your life?

Do you believe it's possible for other people to help shape your life? And if so, in what way or ways?

6. You Had One Promise to Keep

I'm amazed at couples who stand before God, family, and friends on their wedding day, making promises they know they cannot and will never keep because they have chosen to be dishonest. They have a reputation for telling lies. People will say things like…if their lips are moving, they're lying. Who wants a reputation like that? Once you ruin your reputation, it's twice as hard to clean it up; in fact, it's almost impossible. Who could make a promise in front of God, family, and friends when saying their wedding vowels to someone they claim to love? And promising to honor and cherish until death do us part. They knew that, given the first chance, they would cheat because that's what they have always done. I've never understood this, and yet we've seen this happen time and time again.

How did adults get to this point in life that telling a lie, maybe even living a lie, means nothing? Because as children, our parents and family members, as well as others, did their best to teach us how to be good people. And part of that is being told that lying is not good. But what about those lies that are called "white lies." Are these just as bad as a regular lie? Or because it's a lie told to protect someone's feelings; these are okay to tell. But isn't a lie a lie no matter the reason given for telling the lie? It's that slippery slope when we try to defend one's lousy behavior. Can't be done because then the "what if's start popping up and never end. Remember telling the truth is easier than telling a lie. Cause when you tell lies you have to remember what you said so you're not caught in a lie. But then again, if you're not worried about your reputation, what does it matter if you are telling lies…right?

Isaiah 64:8

But now, O Lord, You are our Father, we are the clay, and You our potter; and all of us are the work of Your hand.

So many people play a big role in our upbringing, and this affects us in many ways. From coaches in the sports that we play. They can teach us about sportsmanship and being responsible as well as being respectful to each other. Teachers and others beside family members will have an impact on our lives. And yet somehow some way people will turn out differently than they were taught. How's this happen? Why does this happen? We serve a God who is against telling lies. In fact, He tells us in John 8:44 who the master is of telling lies:

You are of your father the devil, and the desires of your father you want to do. He was a murderer from the beginning, and does not stand in the truth, because there is no truth in him. When he speaks a lie, he speaks from his own resources, for he is a liar and the father of it.

We have all seen two or more people raised in the same house and grow into totally different people. One will grow into someone who is unable to tell the truth, someone who is very shady and lacks any kind of morals, someone whom you're very nervous and uncomfortable to be around. And yet others in this same home will grow into people totally different from the first one described. Again, how does this happen? I believe it's all about choices made by each person. And where do we get those choices from? God. We are molded through the people placed in our lives to teach us right from wrong. We are also taught how to make choices. And yet some will make choices that are totally different than how they were raised.

The choices you have made in your life, be they good or bad, how have these choices impacted your life? Have you ever wondered how the life choices you made impacted those around you? Those same people who gave a little of themselves in helping mold you into becoming the person that you are, good or bad. When they see you, are they proud of who you've become or are they embarrassed? That's something only you can answer and no one else.

Questions for Further Reflection

How many of us know someone who couldn't tell the truth no matter what? And what impact has it had on their lives?

Is there any time telling a lie is ok to do? And if so, when? But later should this person be told they were lied to?

Once your reputation is damaged, be it from telling lies or whatever you did to ruin it, is there anything we can do to repair our reputation or are we forever doomed?

7. The Interchange

Interstate 16 crosses with Interstate 95 in Savannah, Georgia, and this interchange has been under construction, I'm sure, for the last three years or more. The problem is it doesn't seem any closer to being finished since the last time I passed through there. They are working as if someone lost the plans, or maybe they cannot read and understand the plans they are reading. Or perhaps it's because no one was part of the original crew working on this rebuild. Maybe the work crew is new at this type of construction; who knows? But at least they are trying to figure out how this interchange is as they tear it down to rebuild. Who knows, but I know this much, it is taking forever. You're probably wondering what this has to do with Isaiah 64:8, the verse I've based all the devotion on in this book. Everything.

See, I try and look at everyday living and see how it can relate to Scripture and or see how God's hand is in what I'm looking at. Sometimes, I'm slow in seeing what God is showing me, and that's okay because I know I'm not the only one who's lagging in seeing what God is trying to portray. But sooner or later, I'll see what He's showing me. Everything is in God's time, not ours.

Psalm 27:14

Wait on the LORD; bBe of good courage, and He shall strengthen your heart; wait, I say, on the LORD!

Which I know is not as easy as Scripture tells us. No matter who we are, we must wait on the Lord for something to happen in His time. At times, it's more than we can handle, almost to the point of being impossible. If you came to know Christ as your personal Savior as an adult, it would be challenging and take some time, just like this interstate interchange is taking. God will bring people into your life who will help you change how you look at life as a Christian instead of as a nonbeliever. It could be people who knew you as a child and helped you grow into an adult. Or it could be people you have never known that help you grow and change your way of thinking and your outlook on life, just like when tearing apart this interchange and rebuilding it. Some of the original construction crew could be involved or not. But it'll be built with new ways and ideas that'll make it better and safer than before. And this is going to take some time to do. Because God is changing you to become a child of His. But we also must want to change and become a child of God or else nothing will change. Let's look at Isaiah 64:8…

But now O LORD, You are our Father; we are the clay, and You our potter; and all we are the work of Your hand.

No matter when you accept Christ as your personal Savior be you a child or an adult, we are clay in the hands of the Father waiting to be molded into the into the follower he needs us to be. When we allow God to take our hand and lead us instead of trying to take the lead. We'll see great and wonderful things happening by doing so. It's all about serving Jesus and being faithful to Him. We must deny ourselves and pick up our cross to follow Him.

Matthew 16:24-26

Then Jesus said to His disciples, "If anyone desires to come after Me, let him deny himself, and take up his cross, and follow Me. For whoever desires to save his life will lose it, but whoever loses his life for My sake will find it. For what profit is it to a man if he gains the whole world, and loses his own soul? Or what will a man give in exchange for his soul?"

I'm sure in rebuilding this interchange there will be setbacks of all kinds. Issues with the weather and late deliveries of materials needed to complete the job. The same happens with being clay in the Father's hand. But the delays are on us, not the Father. Because "self" gets in the way and causes the delays.

Questions for Further Reflection

Have you ever felt like God was rebuilding you or changing you into being a stronger believer? And if so, how?

Think of one time when you allowed God to use you how He needed to use you and instead of trying to take the lead you followed instead. How did it turn out?

If God is the potter and we are the clay, is it easier to be molded as an adult or as a child into the type of follower that God wants us to be and can use?

What are some of the ways that God will change us as an adult or as a child and do you believe one is harder to do than the other?

8. Great Con Job

We've all met that one person who, whenever we've tried telling them about Jesus or invited them to church, has said they're not interested in church. After visiting more, we find out they grew up in a Christian home and maybe even attended a Christian school. And their parents took them every time the church doors were opened. And when pressed, they will tell you that yes, they were baptized and even went to church camp every summer. But it didn't mean anything to them. They only did this so their parents and the church people would leave them alone. They might have even said as soon as they moved out on their own, they have never been back inside a church and never will!

When I meet people like this, I always wonder what happened to cause them to turn their back on Jesus and walk away. Because if raised in the church, it stands to reason they know the Bible pretty well. We also know that God has placed many people in our lives to mold us and impact us in many ways (Isaiah 64:8). They also know and understand that God allows us to choose to follow Him or not. But we also know that every time we say "no" to God, our hearts grow a little harder. And it gets a bit harder to hear God speak to us. I guess there are some things we will never understand. I've met people like this, and when we part paths, I feel sad for them, knowing there is nothing I can do. But that it's between them and God and no one else. I pray for them, believing that one day before it's too late, they will find their way back to the Lord.

Jeremiah 18:12

And they said, "That is hopeless! So we will walk according to our own plans, and we will every one obey the dictates of his evil heart."

The lives of people who have walked away from the church and God, theirs lives seem to be a mess. Many of them abuse drugs and alcohol and anything else that will hide the pain they are feeling inside. Anything to try and feel that empty void in their lives. But when asked, will always say, "Life is good." A question that comes to mind is: If life is so good and you're doing your own thing, why are you so unhappy? Also, tell us about the good things that the God you serve has done. Because the God I serve and the one you choose not to serve tells me He knew both of us before we were born. Can yours do that?

Jeremiah 1:5

Before I formed you in the womb I knew you; before you were born I sanctified you; I ordained you a prophet to the nations.

People who have been raised in the church as children and then as adults who have chosen to reject Jesus and His teachings instead have chosen to walk away. When on their deathbeds, will they still reject Him or call on Him for forgiveness? We know that God will forgive us with our last breath. But what's changed? You spent your whole life living as you pleased, but now, suddenly, you remember who Jesus is. Maybe they even said often, "I'm a self-made man; I don't need God or anyone." What would your life have been like if instead of running away from Him, you ran towards Him? Again, the God I have chosen to serve has a plan for my life. What plan does the God you've decided to serve have for you?

Jeremiah 29:11-12

For I know the thoughts that I think toward you, says the LORD, thoughts of peace and not of evil, to give you a future and a hope. Then you will call upon Me and go and pray to Me, and I will listen to you.

We all, from time to time, slip and fall when trying as best we can to serve our Savior. After all, we are only human, not perfect by any means. It's at those times that makes the difference between someone who believes in Jesus and someone who's just playing church. I've slipped before, but I want to see what God's planned for me. The hard part after falling is getting back up to keep following Him. The easy thing to do is walk away, rejecting Jesus. Because, after all, little is expected from someone who quits when life gets complicated.

Questions for Further Reflection

Do you know someone who's walked away from the Lord? If so, how can we help them to turn back to Jesus?

Suppose you were raised in the church and have chosen not to attend anymore. How do you overcome that feeling on Sunday morning when you're not where you know you need to be?

You've accepted Jesus as your Savior but later decided you don't want to serve Him and walked away from the church and Him. How will this affect your life in the future? Good or bad or not at all?

9. The Month of May

I look forward to May for a couple of reasons and, at the same time, dread the month for what it stands for. As an over-the-road driver starting this month, you will no longer be required to carry chains. Flowers are beginning to bloom, and the beauty of spring is on its way. There is the smell of fresh-cut grass in the air, and all can hear the sounds of kids playing outside. But come the end of the month, June is a day many would like to forget or wish never happened. But it's a day as I get older that saddens me because I understand the meaning and the sacrifices made by so many. So that we can enjoy the freedoms we have, this day is known by a couple of names…Memorial Day or Decoration Day, but whatever name you choose to call it, it's a day full of memories and sadness. It's a month that has several war movies on TV as well as documentaries about soldiers who went above and beyond what was required of them. But how is someone willing to give their life for someone they don't know? Someone who's not family, someone whom they might have only met at the beginning of boot camp, yet still willing to give their all to save the life of another.

John 15:13

Greater love has no one than this, than to lay down one's life for his friends.

We hear this verse used when soldiers are killed in action when they have paid the ultimate price, the price of their life, so that others could live. By their action, we see this verse lived out before our eyes, which, for me, helps me to understand better the action of Jesus on the cross crying out,

"Father, forgive them, for they do not know what they do."
(Luke 23:34)

The action of the soldier of giving his life so that others may live, if only for that moment and nothing more. Yet, when we read of Christ giving His life on the cross, He gives us, the believer, life for eternity. At the same time, providing forgiveness for those and what they are doing to Him that day, yet through all the pain and suffering and mocking, grants eternal life to one of the thieves. (Luke 23:42)

How does a child play outside, enjoying just a normal summer day as kids do? He becomes someone who joins the military and, at some point in his career, pays the ultimate sacrifice. Who in his life taught him to think of others and to give of oneself? How does one do this? I can't imagine someone willingly giving their life to another. My father was in the military for twenty years, and my brother and I grew up around the military. I could tell there was somewhat of a bond between soldiers, but I wasn't sure what it was. But I learned firsthand what it was when I was in the Air Force. The military teaches you about being part of a team and not as a person. Your actions affect you and those around you who are counting on you. I believe it takes a special person to step in front of harm's way to save a brother's life. Great Wall doesn't hold a candle to what God did for us so we could have eternal life. But more than that, in John 3:17:

For God did not send His Son into the world to condemn the world, but that the world through Him might be saved.

God took the time to mold someone willing to take the place of someone so that person could live…if only for a short time because man cannot give life, unlike God, who can give eternal life. Just like God molded Jesus to go to the cross and take on man's sin so that we might have eternal life, this was Jesus' reason for leaving glory and going to the cross. As a Christian, I sometimes bond with other believers just as I do with fellow veterans. It's hard to explain because you'd have to go through boot camp to understand. And it's the same with this life in Christ. Until you believe and accept Christ as your personal Savior and follow Him in baptism, it's complicated. All you can do is look and wonder, "What's going on?"

Questions for Further Reflection

Would you be willing to give your life to save someone? Not just a loved one but a total stranger?

Have you known someone who gave themselves to protect another person?

How does getting older affect how you look at events in your life? Events in the past and how you look at life going forward?

10. Whose Image? His Image.

Think of any two Christian families that you know and are as identical as possible. Each family has the same number of kids, and their moms volunteer in the community and the church. The dads have good jobs and can spend all their free time with their families. Maybe they are involved in church leadership, nothing special or ordinary with either family. Scripture even tells us that God is the potter, and we are the clay, and that He molds us into what He wants us to be. (Isaiah 64:8) He does this so that we can better serve Him. And we know this because when Jesus called Peter and the others to be His disciples, they dropped what they were doing to follow Him. He told them He'd make them fishers of men.

Mark 1:17

Then Jesus said to them, "Follow Me, and I will make you become fishers of men."

So, we know that God is going to mold us into His image as well as teach us how to be fishers of men. And I'm sure many of us have heard the saying…" Why do bad things happen to good people." I also know and understand that just because we (and our families) are Christian, this doesn't shield us from problems in life or the world. We also don't know what goes on behind closed doors, which could affect how we view and understand life. Not just in ours but others as well. All we can do is look outside and see what's going on. But I have a question, and I believe it's the type of question after talking for a while. We'd be no closer to the answer when we finished than when we began trying to answer the question because we'd be hard-pressed to come up with an answer. Anyone from either family mentioned it doesn't matter which family. In one family, the kids grow up and are successful both in their marriages, the careers they chose, and life in general. They still struggle like anyone else, but nothing like the struggles of the other family. But the other family was not as lucky. Their kids grew up having problems with drugs, divorce, issues of suicide, and just a whole host of other problems. But the parents remain just as faithful through it all.

I've often wondered how the parents deal with this as their family falls apart before their eyes. The bigger question would be how they can remain faithful to God during all this. I'm sure others have seen things like this happening to Christian families, but I always wonder why. And that is my question…Why? I've talked to several Christians about this, and we never really thought about why stuff like this happens. I've also heard non-believers, when they see problems like this in a Christian family, are quick to judge. Saying things like…see you no better than me. But the worst question or commitment a non-believer will make is…why do I need to serve a God who would do something like this to one of His own? Someone always makes a statement like this after a bad storm has destroyed all kinds of homes and lives and left destruction in its path.

How do we, as Christians, answer questions like this? How do we respond in such a way as to lead people to Christ? How do Christians who, before their very own eyes, have seen their families destroyed? How do they even begin to share a positive message about God? Because I'm sure most people would say they wouldn't want to hear anything or any message about a God who'd do something like this to "one of His own." This life we live as Christians sometimes is very difficult to live and serve our Savior. Truth be told, at times, when we see bad things happening to good people, it rocks us to the core, both in how we serve our Lord and, just as equally important, our faith in our God.

Questions for Further Reflection

Do you know Christian parents who, before their eyes, have seen their family destroyed, like what we read about?

Did they keep their faith and still have a strong walk in Christ? Or did it weaken them as it had done their family?

Why do you think God allows bad things to happen to good people?

11. How Are We Impacted?

Have you ever thought about how different people or even sayings you've heard over a lifetime have impacted your life in one way or another? I had breakfast with a Christian friend from church the other day. We try and get together when I'm home on days off. We talk about whatever devotions I'm working on at that time and any ideas I have on new ones, I am thinking about writing. It's just a great time for two brothers in Christ to get together and visit. I have learned over the years that visits like this greatly help me in my walk in Christ. Because we both want the best for each other if you're not doing something like this in your own life, it might be something you might think about doing this, the person you share time with mustn't tell anyone about what's said.

You'd be surprised at how enjoyable this will end up being. But the best part is that you're helping another person without knowing. Sometimes, people are having a rough day but don't like to talk about it, and this is how we help without ever knowing we are. I believe this is part of what Isaiah 64:8 is talking about. God will do something directly to mold or shape us, and we don't know. But one thing we shouldn't do is stand in the way when God is working on us. We should be willing to allow Him to mold us because we have no idea what He has in store for us. We must be careful and not quench the Spirit.

1 Thessalonians 5:17-19

Pray without ceasing, in everything give thanks; for this is the will of God in Christ Jesus for you. Do not quench the Spirit.

I believe, at times, when we visit with someone we don't know very well or not at all, that this is God working through us. I know over the years, I've received so many blessings visiting with drivers at truck stops or even at the docks that, at times, it amazes me how God has used me. And to think none of this would have happened if I'd not been obedient to my Savior. And often, when walking away, I've wondered if I did any good or made a difference in that person's life. But over time, I've learned not to worry about that. Because if I did what I felt led to do, then I did my part, and that's all that matters. Also, God has a way of when you're having a down day that out of nowhere, you'll receive a blessing. And in some small way, you will find out that the person you visited that day made a difference. God's way of letting you know... you've done good.

"I can't hear your actions speaking louder than your words." If you've seen this saying or heard it before, how has it changed how you serve our Lord? If this is the first time you've ever seen this saying, what impact will it have on you? This saying reminds me of the disciples in that no matter how hard they tried to be a strong witness for Jesus. Most times, they blew it. And we are like that in so many ways. This, to me, is how we learn and grow and are slowly becoming how God wants us to serve Him. There is nothing wrong with being "on fire" for Him. But we have to remember we have to wait for Him. Because everything is in His time, and that time is different than our time.

Looking back over my life, the different people who have come and gone are unbelievable. In their way, they have significantly impacted me in one way or another. And have had a small part in who I've become as a husband, a father, and, more importantly, a man of God. I want to think that, in some way, I was able to help them in their life's journey.

Because, after all, that's what life is all about: helping each other in this journey…called life. I'm looking forward to who God will send my way as my life goes along. I know I'm not alone in these thoughts.

Questions for Further Reflection

What are some ways different people who have come and gone in your life have impacted you?

Is it easy to know or challenging to see if you've impacted someone's life without them saying so? And if so, in what way?

What are some of the sayings you've heard that impacted your life?

12. Are We a Doubting Thomas?

Many people throughout our lives will come and go. Many will influence us somehow, and some will even try to drag us down to their level. But we must choose how these people will impact us and our lives. Hopefully, the people who have had a positive influence on us will have given us the knowledge and tools to make good choices. We can see people without knowing how to make good, sound decisions. Or who are easily led astray because they lack the knowledge to make good, strong choices in the people they choose to hang around with. I like to look at the group of men Jesus chose to teach and become His disciples.

There are many guys from different backgrounds and all walks of life. A tax collector, a fisherman, a thief, one who would betray Him, and even one who would sell Him out for a few shiny coins. I've always felt like Jesus put this group together to make it easier for people to identify with and understand that Jesus was looking for imperfect followers. Loyal and wanting to serve Him and give Him their all. Jesus treated them all the same, just as He treats us with love, patience, and understanding. He knows it will take some of us longer than others to get to this point, just as it did for the disciplines.

And some, if not many, will have doubts along the way, just like Thomas. At times, we, too, will doubt our walk with Christ. It's normal, and since we are human, just like the disciplines, it will happen. But it's at those times of doubt that'll make the difference. How we react will show us how strong our walk is. It's very hard to follow someone we've never seen or touched. Unlike the disciples, they were able to do both.

Jesus appeared to the disciples, but Thomas was not with them. Later, when the disciples saw Thomas, they told him about seeing Jesus, how they had seen His nailed scared hands and pierced side. But Thomas said he didn't believe them until he saw Jesus himself. Suppose the disciples teased each other like guys do. But what if Thomas is one of those people who, for no reason, seldom believe anything people tell him? We don't know because Scripture doesn't tell us. It just says Thomas wouldn't believe it until he saw Jesus himself. We read in John where Jesus again appears to the disciplines, and Thomas is with them this time.

John 20:27-29

Then He said to Thomas, "Reach your finger here, and look at My hands; and reach your hand here, and put it into My side. Do not be unbelieving, but believing." And Thomas answered and said to Him, "My Lord and my God!" Jesus said to him, "Thomas, because you have seen Me, you have believed. Blessed are those who have not seen and yet have believed."

It's so easy to relate to the disciplines because they were regular folk just like you and me. Anyone of us at any time can relate to Thomas for being doubtful and not believing until he sees Jesus for himself. But what Jesus says in verse twenty-nine to me is enormous. Here's why. It's harder to believe in something we cannot see, touch, feel, etc. But having the faith to believe in something like this sets Christians apart, believing in something we can't see or touch. It's like a light switch. We know when we flip the switch, the lights will come on. We need to be like that in our walk with Christ. We need to believe that God is always there for us, that it's just a given. But we are human, and Satan is real and doing everything possible to sidetrack us. How many think it could have been Satan messing with Thomas when he doubted the disciples when they told him they had seen Jesus? Or was it just Thomas being doubtful? How many of us can see a little of Thomas in our walk in Christ? I know I can walk in Christ.

Questions for Further Reflection

How can we overcome our doubts and shortcomings when believing what's written in the Bible? Or even our walk in Christ?

Do you think Satan had anything to do with Thomas having a hard time believing what the disciples told him about seeing Jesus? In your own life, have you ever at any time doubted what someone told you about the Bible or their walk in Christ?

Do you sometimes find it hard to believe what's written in the Bible? If so, why?

13. Did You Hear?

How important is listening to God? Will it make a difference one way or another in our walk? What if you're not a Christian and reading this book? Do these questions cause you to stop and think? Or are you just reading the words and not paying attention to what you're reading? You know, Christians do that sometimes…read but don't pay attention to what they're read. Not listening to the preacher as he's preaching the sermon. I have been guilty of doing this a time or two and I'm sure I'm not the only one. As we get into our adult years and get married and start a family and start doing all those adult things. How important will be the advice and guidance that was given to us as kids, which helped mold us and make us who we are? How important will that be? Will that help define us, or do we define ourselves by our actions and how we choose to live life? How important is what we listen to in our lives? I'm sure we all have heard the phase "garbage in garbage out" what's that mean…any ideas? Matthew 13:20 -23 talks about planting seeds. Let's look at that and see what we find.

Verses twenty and twenty-one go together. I'm just going to highlight what the verses say and what they mean for me. These two-verses talk about how seeds are planted in rocky places and because of this have no roots. These words make us feel good for the moment and nothing more. This happens to us a lot in life when we have no core, or character. We're easily lead and get into trouble or find ourselves on the wrong road. Some people will try and blame their parents or where they lived as a child. I agree that some of that could be a factor, but in the end. It's on each and every one of us how we're going to live our lives and no one else. I believe there will always be weak people. But I also believe these same people at some point and time in their lives can find people who will help them in making better choices in life if they let them. And that's the key, wanting to make better decisions.

We've all known someone who has spent their whole lives drinking and doing drugs just living life as one huge party. Maybe even laughed at you for the way you lived your life. But then late in life these party people find out that the life they have chosen isn't as great as they believed it would be. They've accepted Christ as their personal Savior late in life and are doing their best to change their lifestyle and its super hard for them. They need our prayers and guidance to make this change, not our judgement or snide remarks but more importantly words of encouragement. The next verse twenty-two talks about seeds that fall in and among thrones and how this chokes growth. When we allow the pressures of the world to drown out the world of God that's in us, we struggle in our walk in Christ. We stop growing in our faith and are just there. But where is there? I can tell you this much it's not where God wants us to be. We end up being like stale water unable to help anyone let alone ourselves. We don't smell like stale water but we're not far from it. We know what we need to do to change where we're at, all we need to do is act.

And that's the difference between seeds planted in rocky soil and seeds planted in shallow soil. There are some roots but not much, but enough to make a difference. We're able to figure out what's happened and act on it. We'll still need help but not that much because of everyone who's helped us grow and become the person that we are. We draw on that inter strength and that's what helps us to step forward and to move forward. Once we get back on track, we start listening to

God again and finding our way back to where we need to be and were God wants us to be.

And verse twenty-three talks about seeds planted in good soil. This is the man who hears the word and understands it; and he bears much fruit. Is he any better than the other two men. No. When he heard the Word of God it was planted deep within him from the beginning. This could be for any number of reasons. But the one thing we need to remember is that every one of us leans differently. As well as understanding what we read. And we all are going to take a different pace and take a different path to get to where God wants us to end up. Our life experiences help us grow and at the same time we can help others grow who have taken a different path to where God wants them to be to be. So, if you have gotten out of the habit of listening to God today is just as good as any to start listening again.

Matthew 6:6

But you, when you pray, go into your room, and when you have shut your door, pray to your Father who is in the secret place; and your Father who sees in secret will reward you openly.

Questions for Further Reflection

What was some of the best advice you got when you were growing up? And did you follow it right away or after experiencing some hard life lessons?

Looking back on your life to this point what would be one piece of advice you'd give to someone if asked?

If given the chance, would you help someone avoid some of the mistakes you've made, or would you let them make them? If so, why?

14. Eyes to See

I've heard it said that by looking into someone's eyes, you can see who they are. I know that when a doctor looks into our eyes at times, it helps him to figure out what's wrong with us, health-wise. Also, when talking to someone, look straight into their eyes. When doing so, the other person can tell if you're being truthful. But then Scripture also tells us in Matthew 6:22-23:

The lamp of the body is the eye. If therefore your eye is good, your whole body will be full of light. But if your eye is bad, your whole body will be full of darkness. If therefore the light that is in you is darkness, how great is that darkness!

Like normal, it is a very powerful verse with an even more powerful question. How will we answer the question? We all know from time to time we will take our eyes off Jesus and get sidetracked. And we also know that Satan is behind this, getting us sidetracked. All our lives, people who have only wanted the best for us have done all they could to show us how to live. They've taken the time to share their wisdom with us, hoping to keep us from making the same mistakes in life they did. But if we choose not to listen or follow their direction, we will have problems.

How many of us, once we graduated school and got out on our own, decided we knew what was best for us? We landed our first good-paying job, which made it possible to get our place, and we were finally free from having to listen to our parents and their silly and outdated advice. As we lived our lives like we wanted without realizing it, we've stopped going to church, maybe even got in with the wrong crowd. But you know what, we're having a great time, at least we think so.

Some of us will wake up and see we've gotten off track and taken our eyes off Jesus. But for others, it'll take longer, maybe years.

But what's even sadder is that some will never see that the path they've chosen has cost them. It cost them possibly their job or even their family, and all because they took their eyes off Jesus, knowing that doing so was not good. But hey! They lived life to its fullest, and no one would stop them. We know that God will put stuff in our path trying to get our attention, but each time, we reject Him our hearts grow a little bit harder until the day comes when we can't hear Jesus any more or even see Him.

But even if we've reached this point, if we cry out to Jesus, He'll listen to us. It doesn't matter if you were raised in church and have fallen away or have never stepped foot in a church house. You cry out for help, and Jesus will hear. Because up and until we draw our last breath, Jesus is there waiting with His nail-scared hands outstretched, waiting for us to cry out.

I've always felt that if Jesus had called the Religious Leaders of that time, we, the everyday people of today, would have had a hard time understanding the Bible and what Jesus was teaching. Because there wouldn't have been a connection, or it would have been difficult to connect with His teachings. But having called the twelve that He did, we could connect and understand. We can see ourselves in any of the twelve when we mess up, just as those twelve messed up at any given time.

Seeing leaders mess up and own up to it makes them stronger leaders. How many of us can see ourselves being like Thomas and having doubt either in our walk or our faith? Or see ourselves just like Peter, wanting to warm ourselves by the fire. We are willing to do or say anything without any thought, even curse our Savior, to warm our hands. Warned, and still denied our Savior.

How many see us like Judas, selling out Jesus for something shiny? And when we realize what we've done instead of asking Jesus to forgive us, we ask man. That's what Judas did, seeking forgiveness from man. And when a man told him that's your problem, not ours, he took his own life.

For me, Judas is a prime example of what happens when you play church instead of being the church. Judas's sin was no worse than Peter's, who denied Jesus. But Peter knew to ask Jesus for forgiveness, not man. There's a difference between the two; one learned to be the church, the other played church.

There are more examples we can look at where the disciples blew it, but I believe you can see what I'm trying to say. Taking our eyes off the Savior is not good. Losing sight of the Savior's path for us and going on our own will not end well. It'll be a disaster. You know the path you started on but got sidetracked. Why not turn your eyes back on Jesus? Today is never too late.

Philippians 3:14

I press toward the goal for the prize of the upward call of God in Christ Jesus.

Questions for Further Reflection

At any time in your Christian walk have you felt like you have taken your eyes off Jesus? And if so, what happened?

What causes us to lose sight of Jesus and the path He's leading us on?

Have you ever felt like you had a blindfold on when trying to follow Jesus? And if so, what did you do to see again?